# A First Look
# PRAYER

## Lois Rock

### Illustrated by Carolyn Cox

Educational consultant: Margaret Dean

A LION BOOK

Pages 1-12 of this book help explain the meaning of the Lord's prayer, which is given on page 13.

**Our Father**

1  Matthew, chapter 7, verse 7

2  Psalm 23, verses 5 to 6

**in heaven:**

3  Revelation, chapter 4, verse 11

**May your holy name be honoured;**

4  Psalm 99, verses 4 to 5

**may your Kingdom come;**

5  Revelation, chapter 22, especially verse 20

**may your will be done on earth as it is in heaven.**

6  Philippians, chapter 1, verses 3 to 11

**Give us today the food we need.**

7  (Matthew, chapter 6, verses 24 to 34); Psalm 23, verses 1 to 2

**Forgive us the wrongs we have done,**

8  Psalm 51, verses 1 to 13

**as we forgive the wrongs that others have done to us.**

9  (Matthew, chapter 5, verses 43 to 45); Luke, chapter 23, verse 34

**Do not bring us to hard testing**

10  Psalm 119, verses 33 to 40

**but keep us safe from evil.**

11  Psalm 142, verses 1 to 7

12  Matthew, chapter 27, verse 46; Mark, chapter 15, verse 34

13  Matthew, chapter 6, verses 9 to 13; Luke, chapter 11, verses 2 to 4

Text by Lois Rock
Copyright © 1996 Lion Publishing
Illustrations copyright © 1996 Carolyn Cox

The author asserts the moral right to
be identified as the author of this work

Published by
**Lion Publishing plc**
Sandy Lane West, Oxford, England
ISBN 0 7459 3186 3
**Lion Publishing**
4050 Lee Vance Road, Colorado Springs, CO 80918, USA
ISBN 0 7459 3186 3
**Albatross Books Pty Ltd**
PO Box 320, Sutherland, NSW 2232, Australia
ISBN 0 7324 0982 9

First edition 1996
10 9 8 7 6 5 4 3 2 1 0

A catalogue record for this book is available
from the British Library

Library of Congress CIP Data applied for

Printed and bound in Singapore

# Contents

# Introduction
## What is
# Prayer?

For Christians, prayer is a way
of making friends with God.
Christians pray to God when
they are on their own and
also when they are with
other Christians.

Sometimes prayer means
talking. Christians may say
prayers aloud, or just think them.
They believe God always hears.

Sometimes prayer means listening to God.
Christians believe they hear what God says to them
in many ways. It might be that a few words from the
Bible suddenly seem especially important, as if
God is saying them right then and there.
It might be a loud thought—an idea that just won't
go away. It might be that something someone else
says to them seems just like a message from God.

Christians also believe God does things to answer their prayers: for example, they believe that God can take away fear, give joy even in sad times, heal the body, take away worry and give peace instead.

This book will help you understand more about—

- the God to whom Christians pray

- the kind of things they say in their prayers

- the special prayer that Jesus taught

# 1 Let's look at
# Coming home

Think of coming home to a parent
who really loves you—
someone who wants the best for you.

Jesus said that God is like a loving
parent, and God longs to
welcome people.

*Ask, and you will receive.*
*Seek, and you will find.*
*Knock, and the door will be opened*
*to you.*

**From the book Matthew**
**wrote about Jesus**

**Praying to God is like coming home to a loving parent.**

## 2  Let's look at

# A warm welcome

You've been away.
You've come home.
Your family missed you.
How glad they are to see you again.

In the Bible there is a prayer written long
ago by someone who was God's friend.
Christians believe it describes the kind
of welcome God gives anyone.

*Dear God*
*you welcome me into your home.*
*You treat me as a special guest*
*and prepare a party meal for me.*
*The people who hate me*
*look on in surprise.*
*I know you'll look after me*
*all my life.*

**From Psalm 23 of the Bible**

**Prayer is enjoying God's welcome party.**

# 3  Let's look at
# A great big world

Sometimes the world
seems so big:
so high, so wide, so deep.

Something greater than
you has been at work
to make a world like that.

Christians believe that God made everything that exists—in this world, and beyond. The very thought fills them with awe and respect for God.

*Dear God*
*You made the world and*
*everything that lies beyond it.*
*You are great and powerful.*
*I bring you my love and*
*respect.*

**From the last book of the Bible, called Revelation**

**Prayer is talking to God using words of love and respect, for God is greater than anything in this world.**

# 4  Let's look at
# Freshly fallen snow

Have you ever seen
freshly fallen snow,
all smooth and white
and shining?
You hardly dare
breathe:
it is so beautiful,
so perfect.

The way people feel when they see the perfect beauty of freshly fallen snow is just a hint of how Christians feel when they think of God's perfect goodness—God's holiness.

*Dear God*
*You love what is*
*right and good.*
*You are holy.*
*I praise you.*
*I worship you.*
**From Psalm 99 of the Bible**

**Prayer is remembering that God is good and holy and giving God praise and worship.**

# 5 Let's look at
# Longing for summer

In the middle of winter
the world is cold and dark.
Have you ever longed for
summer to come?

Christians believe that God made
a good world. It went bad when
people turned away from God's
goodness.

They believe God came as a
person, Jesus, to make it possible
for God and people to be friends
again. Anyone who becomes
God's friend knows God's
goodness here and now.

One day, Jesus will come back to
reign as God's king and put
everything in the whole world right.

So Christians pray:

*Come, Lord Jesus.*
*Come as king in my life.*
*Come as king in the*
*lives of people in this*
*world today.*
*Come as king of the*
*whole world for ever.*

**From the last book of
the Bible, Revelation**

**Prayer is asking Jesus to come and set up
God's kingdom—in the lives of people
today, and throughout the world for ever.**

# 6  Let's look at
# Dreams come true

Think of good times...
Do you sometimes dream
of a life that's good and
happy all the time? If only
those dreams could come
true!

Christians believe that life
can be good and happy
if people live as God wants—
loving God and loving
other people.

They want to make that dream
come true.

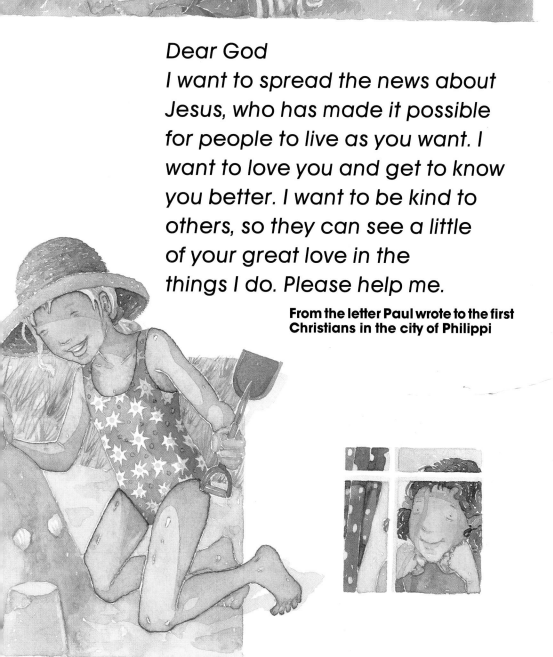

*Dear God*
*I want to spread the news about*
*Jesus, who has made it possible*
*for people to live as you want. I*
*want to love you and get to know*
*you better. I want to be kind to*
*others, so they can see a little*
*of your great love in the*
*things I do. Please help me.*

**From the letter Paul wrote to the first**
**Christians in the city of Philippi**

**Prayer is asking for God's help**
**to learn how to show God's love**
**in the world.**

# 7 Let's look at
# Things we need

What things do you need?
Food … clothes …
somewhere to live …
and so many more things
it would be nice to have!

One day, Jesus was talking to a crowd of people. 'Look at the birds,' he said. 'They don't work and worry to grow their food. Yet God provides what they need.

'And look at the flowers. They don't spin and weave. But the petals God made for them are lovelier than the finest clothes.

'So don't worry about where your food or clothes will come from. God your Father knows you need them. Put God first. And God will provide all these things.'

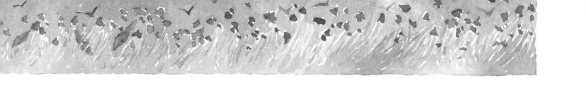

*Dear God*
*You give me everything*
*I need:*
*my food and drink, and*
*a safe place to rest.*

**From Psalm 23 of the Bible**

**Prayer is telling God about everyday
needs, and trusting God for them.**

# 8 Let's look at
# Big mistakes

Have you ever done something really dreadful? Something you can't hide or put right?

Everyone makes mistakes—sometimes big mistakes.

Those who love God feel sad when they know they have done something wrong. They know God loves them, and they have failed to love God back. Saying sorry to God is the first step in putting things right.

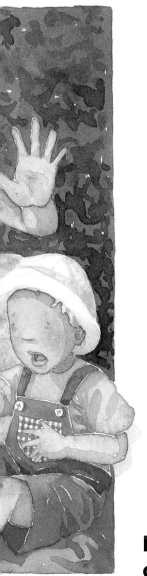

*Dear God,*
*You love me always.*
*Please help me now.*
*I've done something really bad—*
*I'm always getting things wrong.*
*I'm really, truly, sorry.*
*Please give me a new start.*
*Change me from inside,*
*dear God,*
*and make us friends again.*

**From Psalm 51 of the Bible**

**Prayer is asking God to forgive, and accepting the new start God gives.**

# 9 Let's look at
# Enemies

What would you like to do to an enemy?

Jesus reminded people that
God sends rain and sun
to good people and bad
people alike.
He said that his followers
should follow that example,
doing good to people who
treat them well—
and people who treat
them badly.

He said they should pray
for their enemies.

When Jesus' worst enemies
had him put to death, he
prayed for them.

*Dear Father God,*
*Forgive them.*
*They don't know what*
*they are doing.*

**From the books Matthew and**
**Luke wrote about Jesus**

**Prayer is asking God to forgive**
**enemies for the wrong they have**
**done and allow them a fresh start.**

# Friends on a journey

On a long journey,
it's good to have
company:
someone to help you
find the right path,
someone to stop you
wandering
off the path
and getting lost.

Christians believe that
life is like a journey,
with God for
company. As they
learn to listen,
God shows them the
way to go.

*Dear God,*
*Please teach me how you want me to live.*
*I know that's the only way to be really happy.*
*I know it's silly to want to be rich and famous.*
*But I'm a bit afraid people will laugh at me for*
*following you.*
*Please protect me from that.*

**From Psalm 119 of the Bible**

**Prayer is asking God to show**
**the right path through life.**

# 11 Let's look at
# Help

Who will help when the day is going badly?
Who will help when unkind people
want to hurt you?

Christians believe that God will always help, even when things look grim.

*Help me, God, please help me.*
*Let me tell you about the awful*
*things that are happening.*
*My enemies have set a trap*
*for me.*
*No one's stayed to help me.*
*No one cares for me.*
*I'm feeling really gloomy.*
*I'm ready to give up.*
*I don't know what to do next.*
*Please help me.*

**From Psalm 142 of the Bible**

**Prayer is asking God to help in times of trouble.**

# 12 Let's look at
# Feeling lost

Have you ever been out somewhere with someone—and suddenly it seems you've lost them?
You feel terribly alone.

Sometimes, people feel that God has left them on their own. Jesus felt like that when his enemies were killing him. As he died, he said a prayer that he remembered from the Psalms.

It's a very sad prayer, for very sad times, when more and more horrible things seem to be happening.

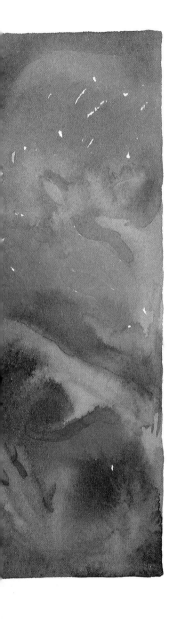

*My God, my God, why have you abandoned me?*

**From the books Matthew and Mark wrote about Jesus**

Jesus died. His friends wept.

Three days later, Jesus' friends said that they had seen him alive again! Christians believe that, through all the sadness, God was there, taking care of all that happened.

**Prayer is crying to God in very sad times, when it seems as if God is doing nothing to help.**

# 13 Let's look at
# Learning

It helps to learn how to write a letter. You learn about the special words people use. You learn about the kinds of things people say. Once you know, it's easier to write your own special letters—your words, your news!

The people who knew Jesus on this earth wanted to learn to pray to God as easily as Jesus did. They asked Jesus to teach them. He gave them this prayer.

*Our Father in heaven:*
*May your holy name be honoured;*
*may your kingdom come;*
*may your will be done on earth*
*as it is in heaven.*
*Give us today the food we need.*
*Forgive us the wrongs we have done,*
*as we forgive the wrongs that*
*others have done to us.*
*Do not bring us to hard testing*
*but keep us safe from evil.*

**From the books Matthew and Luke wrote about Jesus**

Today, Christians call it 'the Lord's prayer'.
Many Christians say these special words
of Jesus as a prayer, and it helps them
with all their prayers.

**Christians learn to pray to God
from the prayer that Jesus taught.**

# What is prayer?

1    Praying to God is like coming home to a loving parent.

2    Prayer is enjoying God's welcome party.

3    Prayer is talking to God using words of love and respect, for God is greater than anything in this world.

4    Prayer is remembering that God is good and holy and giving God praise and worship.

5    Prayer is asking Jesus to come and set up God's kingdom—in the lives of people today, and throughout the world for ever.

6    Prayer is asking for God's help to learn how to show God's love in the world.

7    Prayer is telling God about everyday needs, and trusting God for them.

8    Prayer is asking God to forgive, and accepting the new start God gives.

9    Prayer is asking God to forgive enemies for the wrong they have done and allow them a fresh start.

10    Prayer is asking God to show the right path through life.

11    Prayer is asking God to help in times of trouble.

12    Prayer is crying to God in very sad times, when it seems as if God is doing nothing to help.

13    Christians learn to pray to God from the prayer that Jesus taught.